CW00822296

Title:

The Challenges and Joys of Parenting Kids With Down Syndrome

Nicole J. Smiths

The Joy and Challenges of parenting kids with Down Syndrome.

Copyright

The Joy and Challenges of parenting kids with Down Syndrome.

Table of contents

CHAPTER ONE 1

Introduction

As parents of a child with Down syndrome, we've learned to embrace the joys that come with this condition. Our daughter has brought so much happiness into our lives, and we've come to appreciate the little things that much more.

Kids with Down syndrome are often known for their sweet and gentle disposition, and ours is no exception. She has a smile that lights up a room, and she's always happy to give hugs. We've also been blessed with a strong bond that we know won't be broken.

We know that raising a child with Down syndrome comes with its own set of

challenges, but we wouldn't change a thing.

We've learned so much about patience, love, and resilience, and we've become stronger as a family because of it.

1. What is Down Syndrome

Down Syndrome is a hereditary condition that causes gentle to serious physical and formative issues.
Individuals with Down Syndrome are brought into the world with an additional chromosome. Chromosomes are heaps of qualities, and your body depends on having the perfect number of them. With Down syndrome, this additional chromosome prompts a scope of issues that influence you both intellectually and genuinely.

Down Syndrome is a hereditary condition that happens when there is an additional duplicate of a particular chromosome:

chromosome 21. The additional chromosome can influence an individual's

actual elements, mind, and generally speaking turn of events. It likewise improves the probability of some medical issues.

Down Syndrome is a deep-rooted condition. Even though it can't be restored, If your kid makes them get, the right consideration almost immediately can have a major effect in assisting them with carrying on with a full and significant life.

Down Syndrome can influence an individual's mental capacity and the actual development, cause changing

formative contrasts, and present a higher gamble of some medical issues.

Medical services experts can utilize a progression of screenings and tests to distinguish Down syndrome previously or after birth.

Down disorder happens in around 1 in every 700 children conceived.

Types of Down Syndrome

There are maybe one or two types of Down syndrome:

1. *Trisomy 21*: This is the most well-known type, making up around 95% of cases. It happens when individuals have 47 chromosomes in every cell rather than 46. A mistake in cell division called nondisjunction causes trisomy 21. This blunder leaves a sperm or egg cell with an additional duplicate of chromosome 21 preceding or at origination.

2. *Mosaic Down condition*: This type happens in around 2% of individuals with Down syndrome. A portion of the child's

chromosomes will contain an additional duplicate of chromosome 21, while different cells will have the run-of-the-mill two duplicates. Youngsters have fewer

trademark highlights of the condition, contingent upon the number of cells with one or the other 2 or 3 duplicates of chromosome 21.

3. *Translocation Down Syndrome*: This makes up around 3% of instances of Down Syndrome. This type happens when part of chromosome 21 severs during cell division and joins to another chromosome, generally chromosome 14. The presence of this additional piece of chromosome 21 causes some Down Syndrome qualities. An individual with a movement has no exceptional actual highlights, however, they are bound to have a youngster with an additional chromosome 21.

Characteristics of Down Syndrome

People with Down syndrome regularly have particular actual elements, one-of-a-kind

medical problems, and changes in mental turn of events.

Physical features
Some common actual characteristics of Down syndrome can include:

 * eyes that inclination vertical
* skin folds on the internal corner of the upper eyelid
* white spots on the iris
* low muscle tone
* Small stature and a short neck
* A flat nasal bridge
* single, profound wrinkles across the focal point of the palms
* A Protruding tongue
* Little hands and feet

Developmental delays

Individuals with Down syndrome for the most part have mental advancement profiles

that propose gentle to direct savvy handicap. However, cognitive development and intellectual ability are highly variable.

Individuals with Down syndrome likewise experience learning challenges that lead to formative postponements. An individual with Down Syndrome has a particular example of mental and social highlights. These contrast based on what is seen in normally creating youngsters and kids with different reasons for scholarly handicaps.

Kids with Down syndrome frequently arrive at formative achievements somewhat later than their friends. They might be delayed to sit, turn over, and stand.

There may likewise be a postpone in coordination and fine coordinated movements (developments involving little muscles in the hands and wrists). These abilities can find an opportunity fostered after the kid gains net coordinated

movements, which include the development of the entire body.

Improvement of communicating in and getting a handle on a language may likewise take surprisingly lengthy. With this expressed, individuals with Down syndrome in the end meet a large number of these achievements.

Individuals with Down syndrome may likewise experience:

* Hardships with consideration
* An inclination to make misguided decisions
* impulsive behavior

With commitment and normal treatment, the vast majority with Down disorder can go to class and become dynamic individuals from the local area.

CHAPTER TWO 2

Causes and diagnosis of Down Syndrome

Many variables add to Down syndrome, yet the commonness is higher in older pregnant people. There may be a higher chance if a pregnant person is over age 35.

A pregnant individual at age 25 has around oy 10ssibilitiestoconsideringg a youngster with Down syndrome. At age 40, the frequency turns out to be around 1 of every 100.

Human cells typically contain 23 sets of chromosomes. One chromosome in each pair comes from your dad, the other from your mom.

All cells in the body contain qualities, which have a particular code or set of guidelines for making the cells. These qualities sit inside chromosomes in the cell core.

Down syndrome results when strange cell division including chromosome 21 happens. These cell division irregularities bring about an additional halfway or full chromosome 21. This extra hereditary material is answerable for the trademark highlights and formative issues of Down Syndrome.

There are no known conduct or ecological elements that reason Down syndrome.

Is Down Syndrome genetic?

Generally speaking, Down Syndrome isn't acquired and doesn't run in families. However Down syndrome comes from the actual qualities, this is for the most part because of blunders between a sperm and an egg when the hereditary data that frames

a youngster first consolidates and duplicates.

Down syndrome can have connections to hereditary qualities. There might be a few connections between guardians of an individual with translocation Down syndrome and their probability to have more kids with Down syndrome at times.

At the point when balanced translocations are inherited, the mother or father has some modified hereditary material from chromosome 21 on another chromosome, yet no extra hereditary material.

This implies the person has no signs or side effects of Down syndrome, however, can give an unbalanced translocation to kids, causing Down syndrome in the youngsters.

Risk factors

A few guardians have a more serious risk of having a child with Down Syndrome. Risk factors include:

* *Progressive maternal age.* A lady's possibility of bringing forth a kid with Down Syndrome increments with age because more seasoned eggs have a more serious risk of inappropriate chromosome division. A woman's risk of conceiving a child with Down syndrome increases after 35 years of age. However, most children with Down syndrome are born to women under age 35 because younger women have far more babies.

*   *Being transporters of the hereditary translocation for Down syndrome.* All kinds of people can give the hereditary

translocation for Down Syndrome to their children

*   *Having had one child with Down syndrome.* Guardians who have one youngster with Down syndrome and guardians who have a movement themselves are at expanded risk of having one more kid with Down syndrome. A hereditary guide can assist guardians with evaluating the risk of having a second youngster with Down syndrome.

Diagnosis

People with a higher chance of having a child with Down syndrome might receive screenings and diagnostic tests.
There are two categories of screening tests that doctors can perform.

Prenatal screens can estimate the probability of a person having a baby with

Down syndrome and justify further tests, but they do not diagnose Down syndrome.

Diagnostic tests can definitively tell whether a fetus will have the condition and identify certain abnormalities.

Screening tests

Due to the increased chances of having a child with Down syndrome, people aged 30–35 or older might receive genetic screenings during pregnancy.

These tests are completely optional, and not everyone will choose genetic screening while pregnant.

There are several screening tests, which include:

* Nuchal translucency testing: At 11–14 weeks, an ultrasound can measure the clear

space in folds of tissue behind the neck of a developing fetus.

* Triple screen or quadruple screen: At 15–18 weeks, this test measures the quantities of various substances in the pregnant person's blood.
Integrated screen: This combines results from first-trimester blood and screening tests, with or without nuchal translucency, with second-trimester quadruple screening results.

* Cell-free DNA: This is a blood test that analyzes fetal DNA present in the pregnant person's blood.

Genetic ultrasound: At 18–20 weeks, doctors combine a detailed ultrasound with blood test results.

Screening tests cannot confirm whether Down syndrome is present.

Screening is a cost-effective and less invasive way to determine whether doctors may need to order further diagnostic testing.

Diagnostic tests

Diagnostic tests are more accurate at detecting Down syndrome.

A healthcare professional will usually perform such tests inside the uterus.

However, diagnostic tests can increase the risk of:

*miscarriage

* fetal injury

* preterm labor

Diagnostic tests include:

* Chorionic villus sampling: At 9–11 weeks, a doctor might use a needle inserted into the cervix or the abdomen to take a tiny sample of the placenta for analysis.

* Amniocentesis: At 14–18 weeks, a doctor may insert a needle into the abdomen to obtain a small amount of amniotic fluid for analysis.

* Percutaneous umbilical blood sampling: After 20 weeks, the doctor may insert a needle into the abdomen to take a small sample of blood from the umbilical cord for analysis.

Down syndrome can also be diagnosed after a baby is born by inspecting their:

*physical characteristics
* blood
* tissue

Treatment

There is no specific treatment for Down syndrome. People who have the condition will receive care for any health problems, as other people do.

However, healthcare professionals may recommend additional health screening for issues common to people with the condition.

The National Institute of Child Health and Human Development recommends early intervention with specialized programs to help a person maximize their potential and prepare to take an active role in the community. Early intervention may help improve outcomes for people with Down syndrome.

Working with a team of specialists can provide stimulation and encouragement to the child as they grow. This can include many specialists in different fields to help the person develop. These specialists may include:

 * physicians
* physical therapists
* speech therapists
* Special educators
* occupational therapists
* social workers

Children with specific learning and developmental difficulties may be eligible for educational support in a public or specialized school.

Children with Down syndrome are entitled to an appropriate educational environment that fits their needs, often with additional support to help them integrate and make progress.

Some children will make use of an Individualized Education Program (IEP), which various specialists will support.

CHAPTER THREE 3

Raising your kids with Down Syndrome in the 21st Century.

Every family has its joys, stresses, and challenges, but when you have a child with Down syndrome, things look a little different. Besides juggling school, music lessons, sports, and jobs, you typically have a lot of extra visits with doctors and therapists in the mix.

Like most children, kids with Down syndrome tend to do well with routine. They also respond better to positive support than discipline. Keep both of those things in mind as you try the following tips

Do all the common kids' things:

. Give your kid errands around the house. . . Simply split them up into little advances and show restraint.

. Have your youngster play with different children who do and don't have Down disorder.

. Keep your assumptions high as your kid attempts and learns new things.

. Make time to play, read, have a good time, and go out together.

. Support your kids in doing everyday assignments all alone.

For everyday activity:

. Make a day-to-day everyday practice and stick to it overall quite well. For instance, the morning may be "get up/have breakfast/clean teeth/get dressed."

. Assist your kid with changing, starting with one action and then onto the next with exceptionally clear signals. For more

youthful children, seeing an image or singing a melody can help.

. Use pictures to create an everyday timetable your youngster can see.

To assist your kid with school, you may:

.Abstain from saying "That's wrong" to correct mistakes. Instead, say, "Attempt it once more." Offer assistance assuming that it's required.

As you work with specialists, advisors, and educators, center around your kid's requirements as opposed to on the condition.

Take a look at what your kid is learning at school and check whether you can work those examples into your home life.

At the point when you converse with your kid, keep it basic - - the fewer advances, the better. For instance, attempt "Kindly put

your night robe on," rather than "Alright, it's sleep time. We should get your teeth cleaned, face washed, night robe on, and choose a few books."

Have your kid echo headings once again to you so you realize you've been perceived. Name and discuss things your youngster appears to become amped up for.

Give Your Child Some Control

All children genuinely must feel like they have some command over their lives. It's considerably more significant for youngsters with Down syndrome, and it's one method for assisting them with carrying on with a satisfying life. For instance, you can:

Allow your child to pursue decisions when it's a good idea to. This can be essentially as basic as allowing them to pick what garments to wear.

Permit them to face sensible challenges. This is a test each parent faces. You want to safeguard your kids, yet additionally, let them see what they can deal with.

Support them in taking care of issues, similar to how to manage an issue with companions or move toward an issue at school. You don't need to fix it for them, yet assist them with doing it without anyone's help.

Great Tips on raising kids with Down Syndrome

Bringing up a kid with Down Syndrome (DS) can be challenging and it is entirely expected for guardians to go through sensations of nervousness and dread.

Higher possibilities of unexpected issues, for example, innate heart deserts, resistance problems, gastrointestinal deformities, and spinal issues can add to the difficulties of really focusing on a youngster with DS. Fortunately, there is a lot of help accessible

for guardians and early intercession can essentially work to their satisfaction. With enough help, love, and support, kids with DS can acquire freedom, and proceed to lead a rich and satisfying life.

Here are a few ways to raise a youngster with Down Syndrome

1. *Spend time, talk, and play with them*

Like different youngsters, those with DS additionally need mental and social excitement. You really should make time to play and mess around with them. They

additionally need their companion bunch. Thus, present and make them play with kids who might have DS. Keep some time to the side regularly to converse with your youngster on different issues, including their school, companions, or whatever else they might wish to discuss. You ought to likewise converse with them about current

undertakings and other consumer issues. Keep the discussion basic and answer their inquiries sincerely.

2. *Establish an everyday practice*

Routine is vital to each kid and consistency can hugely comfort. For a kid with DS, it very well may be much more significant and any deviations can disturb. In this way, ensure that you adhere to the daily practice and roll out no improvements. Simultaneously, a few interruptions are

inescapable, for example, the visit of visitors or the conclusion of their school, which can endanger their standard daily schedule. In such cases, one ought to set up the youngster well ahead of time.

It tends to be through stories or viewable signs making sense of the approaching interruptions. Incessant redundancies or conversations of the occasion will

intellectually set up the youngster to anticipate the occasion.

3. *Use various guides for their general Development*

Kids with DS can benefit gigantically from an advanced learning approach, however, one should figure out how to tailor their showing helps and language. Utilize clear, straightforward, and open language and put

accentuation on visual education help. Add pictures, bright graphs, and recordings to support instruction. They additionally benefit from dull education. At last, have persistence. Your kid might need to invest additional energy and time to gain proficiency with his/her lesson.

4. *Helping around the house*

Include your child in ordinary exercises by giving him/her basic tasks to do around the

house. Begin with showing them their everyday obligations, from taking care of the dishes to cleaning after themselves. As they become older, the degree of trouble of the undertakings can be gradually raised to incorporate tasks like tidying up their room or assisting with clothing. These exercises are planned to construct their opportunity and confidence. Yet, make sure to keep your

directions straightforward and straightforward.

5. Reinforce acceptable behavior

Kids advance acceptable conduct from the reaction of their folks. You can build up acceptable conduct by commending appropriate conduct. Kids with DS answer all the more decidedly to viewable prompts. Thus, a graph can frequently work better to improve their instruction.

6. Set long-haul objectives. Keep them practical

Putting forth objectives can be useful to keep one on target. In any case, it's likewise critical to keep these objectives practical. Your youngster will get some margin to arrive at specific formative objectives. Long-haul objectives are likewise useful when brief mishaps happen. It advises us

that we should finish what has been started and search for options when confronted with an obstacle.

While raising a youngster with DS, it's consistently vital to recall that your kid is on their way. It might vary for different youngsters, however, it is similarly as important and delightful as some other kids. Thus, commend your kid's accomplishments, perceive their achievements, and watch them blossom and flourish.

The Joy and Challenges of parenting kids with Down Syndrome.

The Joy and beauty of Down Syndrome

1. Your child is a child first. You are not bringing forth a "Down Syndrome" child. You are bringing forth your child, a special person who will bear a likeness to you and your family notwithstanding a few comparable highlights to others with Down

disorder. It's astonishing how much my two kids look like each other even though one has Down disorder and the other doesn't. You don't need to adore Down disorder to cherish your child. Center around the life - -, not the mark.

2. Your child will in any case accomplish typical achievements. On the off chance that you have kin or companions who had babies close to a similar time you had yours, you might end up falling into the examination trap. Try not to contrast your child with ordinarily creating infants. All things being

equal, begin posting the things that your child has achieved. Try not to lessen your youngster's wonderful and triumphant field of daisies by contrasting it with the closest mountain. The achievements could take somewhat longer, however, when they at last occur.?
The festival is a lot happier.

3. There is a great deal of support and help available. There is general support for a parent with an extraordinary youngster's needs. For instance, you can enlist your child in your state's Early Intervention (EI) program as soon as about a month and a half old. early mediation signifies "mediating right off the bat in a kid's life to empower development and improvement. Various experts are engaged with giving EI administrations, remembering experts for coordinated abilities, language and correspondence, learning procurement, and social-profound turn of events." Your kid

will start treatments to help her arrive at achievements quicker and accurately
This will set great ways for future learning.

4. There is a lot of beauty in Down Syndrome. Frequently my girl's excellence blows my mind: Sparkling almond-molded eyes that are a similar variety as her Daddy's, an enthralling grin that frequently prompts chuckling so irresistible that the hardest of hearts will liquefy accordingly, little hands that rush to look for underhandedness and afterward sign for pardoning, a charming hole between her toes that is ideal for wearing shoes.

Permit your cliché reality to disintegrate and genuinely get to realize the individual secret under the mark.

5. Your child will encounter a large number of feelings. You could hear somebody say

that your child will be "consistently cheerful," which can cause your child to

appear to be some way or another less human. In any case, your child will show a wide range of temperaments - - blissful, miserable, senseless, irate, whiny, crazy, charmed - - equivalent to some other individual. The

6. Frustration can be a decent reason to get innovative with your education approach. Embrace the one-of-a-kind disappointments you might confront and understand that each kid advances unexpectedly. For instance, if your kid experiences issues conveying verbally, show her gesture-based communication. "Communication via gestures is a brilliant device that permits even tiny kids to put themselves out there."

7. Down Syndrome won't define your kid's whole existence. The gigantic piece of

information won't eclipse for what seems like forever and will ultimately slide out of the spotlight of day-to-day life. You will

have terrible days that don't have anything to do with a finding. You will chuckle in the future and cry in the future about different things. You will partake in a ton with your kid that doesn't have anything to do with

chromosomes or treatment or regular checkups.

Conclusions

Individuals with Down syndrome are becoming increasingly integrated into society and community organizations, such as schools, health care systems, work forces, and social and recreational activities. Individuals with Down syndrome possess varying degrees of cognitive delays, from very mild to severe. Most people with Down syndrome have cognitive delays that are mild to moderate.

Due to advances in medical technology, individuals with Down syndrome are living longer than ever before. In 1910, children with Down syndrome were expected to survive to age nine. With the discovery of antibiotics, the average survival age

increased to 19 or 20. Now, with recent advancements in clinical treatment, most

particularly corrective heart surgeries, as many as 80% of adults with Down syndrome

reach age 60, and many live even longer (Down syndrome, 2018). More and more Americans are interacting with individuals with Down syndrome, increasing the need for widespread public education and acceptance.

The Joy and Challenges of parenting kids with Down Syndrome.

Parenting kids with Down Syndrome can be challenging, but it's also filled with joys that other parents may not experience. Every child with Down Syndrome is unique, so there's no one-size-fits-all answer to the question of how to care for them.

The best way to care for your child is to learn as much as you can about Down

Syndrome and to connect with other parents of kids with Down Syndrome. There are many organizations and communities available that can offer support and advice.

Above all, enjoy your child! They are a blessing, and you are one of the lucky ones to have them in your life.

Printed in Great Britain
by Amazon

37245832R00030